Love's Musings

Love's Musings

Jeanine A. Rogers

5 POINT VISION, LLC
FROM CONCEPTION TO CREATION

Contents

"'Tis better to have loved and lost than never to have loved at all."
~Alfred Tennyson

Thank you to my village for loving me.

1

Sunshine on a Cloudy Day

I want

I want to be your partner
your sidekick
your confidant and friend
your support
encouraging you to win
your laughter after a long day
your lady
your lover
the one like no other
your cheerleader
your coach
through everything
your hope
your help
your magnet for wealth
your lifeline
your connection
a recipient of your direction
I want to be your biggest fan
your muse
your admirer
your right hand
I want to be all of this to you
because it is what you are to me.

Longing

I've learned you can't rush time
Neither can you slow it down
Yet time seems to move so slowly
when you're not around

In anticipation of our next time
I often venture into my mind
Where each moment and memory reside
Hearts and spirits and souls intertwined

Here I find myself at ease
Willing to wait for what I need
Though it seems an eternity in a week
Hoping I'll have enough time to speak
With the one who understands my soul
I long for the chance to kiss touch and hold
Bringing comfort to the one who's stories console
Every ounce of doubt in my mind
In your presence I'm at peace, sublime
Fulfilled beyond the highest measure
I cherish every moment we spend together
As our lives connect with divine design
In an embrace of love, purpose aligned.

Love Defined

I love the way you flow
I love the way I grow when I'm with you
I love the way you show me God's plan of what to do

I made mistakes before
but no one has ever loved into being more

I love the way you speak to my mind
I love the way our spirits intertwine

And how you dissect every word that comes out
I love the way you take me out
To places unknown

I love the way I've grown being with you
I love our time together, planned or impromptu
I love the way you hold my hand
I love the way you never allow me to be less than who I am
I love the way you listen
I love the way you grab my heart's attention
I love the way you teach me
I love the way you reach me
I love that you allow God to complete me
I love every little thing you do to show me you care
I love the way you touch my hair
I love the way we connect and I love the way our souls
intersect at a common place on the way to greater

I love you now
but I know I'll love you more later
because of who we are becoming
I love the way you keep me running
back for more

I love the way you make me deal with those ugly things
I love how your correction is never mean
I love the way you've learned my ways
I love the time you've invested into my daughter's days
I love the new meaning I have in life
I love that I can be happy by your side
I love the way you kiss me by surprise
I love the feel of you between my thighs

More than anything I love what I see
when I look into your eyes
I love that in you God's love resides

Love Unfolds

In the morning with the rising sun
My mind floats to the mystery you've undone
In revealing the very essence of you
If I'm Cinderella, this is my dream come true

Your voice elevates to another plane
My soul is touched each time you say my name
Naivety is the farthest from my mind
In order for great things to grow, it will take time
And time is an investment of sacrifice

Long days lead to long nights, unwinding together
Kissing away the problems you've endeavored
Knowing it's for God's glory that we've been connected
Joy is a bonus that comes as we're perfected in His love

Have you come to experience the totality of
God's spirit manifested
In the companion who was arrested
By the voice that spoke to the innermost part of her soul
Walk with me, my sweet, let's watch love unfold...

Joy Personified

One day I met joy personified...

I could tell from one look in your eyes
That you were set apart
I knew from the start that this was no dream
Although as perfect as it may seem
This was my new reality
Part of God's plan for me
And for you

It was not by chance that our two paths crossed
Before that moment such a life was just a thought
Now we walk side by side down this new road
Watching our lives and love unfold
There are so many stories left to be told
We will look back on that day when we are old
And be filled with wonder at God's grand design
For life began anew when you entered mine....

Déjà Vu

I just had **déjà vu**
Of me thinking of you
Could it be at another time
I was yours and you were mine?
Or was the master plan that we would be intertwined
At such a time as this?
I would be remiss if I didn't long for such meaning
In a world where people are constantly dreaming
Of a connection so rare
It's in the way you stare into my eyes
My whole body is hypnotized
By your close proximity
Yet there's nowhere else I'd rather be
Than in your space, caressing your face
Sharing a warm embrace and thoughts laced
With the wonders of the almighty
Captured by the spirit of liberty
Free to relax and enjoy the ride
From this my heart shall not hide...

No Limit

Sometimes you can't let go...
But destiny would have it another way
I still recall the first time you looked my way
It was as if angels began to play just for me
For here was a man who could see the real me
Before I knew who I truly was,
you showed me what I could be
Countless hours we spent sharing dreams,
who knew what it would come to mean years later
It wasn't until I was grown that I realized
the look in your eyes was love
Genuine friendship that could only come from above
You moved me....

Moved me to smile, dance, sing a new song
It's funny I see that all along I cared
Locked away inside my heart were feelings
that never dared to surface
Oh but every minute was worth it...
You helped me to see what it could be
And even though it is not currently
The truth is your love changed me,
rearranged me to see that love has no time limit
From day one, my heart was always in it
As it forever will be, my baby and me....

Miss You More

I miss your scent, your touch and kiss...
How much longer must I reminisce
On the last time you caused an explosion
Every moment with you replayed in slow motion
From the tender touch to the gentle grab
Exploring the treasure you were meant to have

I want to share in this ecstasy
Of hearts and souls connecting organically
I yearn for the one who puts my mind at peace
How I long to be your sweetest release...

Missing You

It is agony not having you here

How I long to hold you near

And inhale all of you

Caress my back the way you do

Reacquaint our bodies and minds

Unleash the anticipation of loves incline

Let me arch my back and surrender to your desires

Come to me, I promise I won't get tired

I want to show you how much I miss your touch

Whisper so softly I've missed you so much

As we become one wave in the space of life's ocean

Our souls connect in an infinite devotion

Dreaming

Just know that you are missed immensely
How I long to be laying up against the
Strength of your manhood
To listen to the beat of your heart
As we share ideas of future starts
To feel the sensuality of your eyes
In this time I've come to realize
You stir up the depths of my soul
I want to be the one who you hold
When the days are long and the demanding great
I pray God gives us the time to make
Memories that will last throughout time
Until then these dreams run through my mind...

In Every Season

S easons change
    Mad things rearrange...

But don't let the change in weather
Lead you to question whether
You still are in the right position
You are where you are supposed to be...listen

No one can bring what I can to you
In the deepest and darkest time I will always be true
don't box me into one dimension
Allow me to show you another extension

Of my ability to transform
Into a butterfly reborn

In everything I give thanks and
I pray through the circumstance
Continue to allow the chance
For me to be your best friend
Not for titles sake, but for us to win
Because we are strong apart, but
Even mightier together
Connecting for us allows us to sever
Every hold the enemy tries to bring
Together we can withstand anything

If you believe God and what He said
All those other thoughts, bury them dead
Because a three fold cord is not easily broken

God between us brings words that need not be spoken
I want to give all of myself it's true
In every season, you are there for me
And I am there for you

Let us not let time or distance be a shield
Pausing what we are supposed to build
Place your heart and hand in mine
Let's walk this journey together for all time.

Last Night

Last night I longed for you
As I lay in my bed I had thoughts of you
Doing all the things you do
Being you and only you
Making me laugh
Making me smile
Boy you made my life worthwhile
And after a time
I realized you could never be mine

I remember when we used to hold hands
Together we would dance
I can still feel the romance
We had when given a chance
Now I always see your face
I can feel your embrace
I remember times we bared our souls
Oh, I'm losing control
Cause I miss you
The little things you do
Making me laugh
Making me smile
You made my life worthwhile
And after a time
I realized you could never be mine

Oh, how many times do you find a love so sweet
I don't know if I'll ever meet

A man like you
A love so true
I wonder if ever you're gonna look my way
And realize what you've thrown away
The day will come when you will see
I was all of the woman you would ever need

I love you still inside my heart
Though we have to be apart
I'll never ever ever stop loving you
And the little things you do
When you're
Making me laugh
Making me smile
You made my life worthwhile
And after a time
I knew it in my mind
My heart was so blind
And after a time
I realized you could never be mine.

Restore

I still get excited when I hear your voice
I am thrilled when you want to talk
and share with me by choice
That bond between us is strengthened every time
You share with me a piece of your mind
When you are gone a part of me is missing
Not because you complete me but
because I want to be a part of your vision
Something in the spirit comes alive
When we rest in each other's heart with truth as our guide

You want to know my frustration?
It's when I can't feel your vibration
Since the moment you reached out and touched my heart
The power of my soul received a jump start
If I ever seem far away
I am simply searching for the right words to say
Trying to find the path to enter your world
I desire to be your go to girl
For happiness and pain
Sunshine and rain

Forgive me if I struggle through life at times
I only want to make the most of this time we've been given
To hold you near and inspire you to keep living
As you inspire me to be
The woman you awoke and empower me to be

Thank you

Thank you for sharing your love with me
You have brought me to a place of destiny
Unraveled through every word and touch
I've come into knowing myself as more
than enough

In just a look from your eyes
I am still surprised at the intensity I feel
The connection between us is unreal
Yet it is so on time
Swimming in a sea of sublime elation
There is no worthy summation
Of what you've brought to my heart
With your powerful masculinity
you gave me a jump start
Charging me up for greatness to be revealed
Completely surrendered with God at the wheel

Some things happen by chance
But this is more than a mere circumstance
I only hope that I can always be
All that you are and more for me

Easy

Sometimes love comes in an instant
Colliding with the heart although it is resistant
It comes through like after a storm passes over
Transforming clouds into rays of sunshine restored
That's how love came to exist
In a world where love was erased from the list

From an introduction
To glances of seduction
Where did this come from?
This was just supposed to be fun...

Laughter intertwined
with soulful connections in time
A subtle glance
Sparked thoughts of romance
Can it be this easy?
Conversations from morning to evening

I look for you in the quiet of the morning
Drift to sleep with the safety of yearning
Just to be in the comfort of your presence
Can one fall in love with another's essence?
Compliments sown generously make
Smiles come effortlessly
Wondering what would it be like
To share space continuously
Opportunity knocks at inopportune times
And imagination advances steadily from behind

In another dimension we coexisted
Souls travel across generations to revisit
Purity of love in the form of friendship
Morphed into admiration and genuine contentment
Sometimes love comes easy

My Angel

You see me
In my entirety
The parts I try to hide
The hurts I push aside
You see beyond my smile
Never judging all the while
Building my inner self
I don't have to ask for help
Our connection lets you know
Just what I need to grow
With you by my side
My soul no longer cries out
For understanding
Your presence in my life
Relives the pressure that life is demanding
And I'm again at rest in your love
My angel sent to me from above...

Falling

They say people fall in love
But maybe they leap
Maybe they jump

Perhaps it's the rush of emotions that catches one
off guard
Like a plane taking off

Anticipation at the thought of where it will go
Excitement as you board the carrier with your heart
Strap in, you're going for a ride
In case of emergency, argument or issue
Put on your oxygen mask first
And in the event of an unexpected landing
Keep a life jacket close so that you don't drown
in your sorrow

Ready to go, looking out the window toward love
Cleared for take off to bliss
The engine revs and speed picks up
Conversations deepen and prayers are spoken
As the wheels lift your heart drops
and you wonder will this work

Ascension, the beauty of the sky becomes the canvas
Oh a bump, what was that?
Just a point of misunderstanding
Align with the horizon....
keep the focus...
turbulence resolved

Then you glide to 10,000 feet
Safe to relax, move around
and feel the joy of suspension in mid air
Cruising altitude reached.
Enjoy the ride of love!

2

Some Days I Reminisce

Late Night

Late night...

Some sit by candlelight

others stay up and fight

yet I sit here and write

and delight at the sound of the key

strokes across the screen

mind racing, contemplating

the things of the past

sometimes I wonder why it didn't last

or should I even ask

Late night...

the time when my mind takes flight

soaring over what could be and what has already been

A blank canvas is my life and I have the pen

yet what shall I write in the book of life this

Late night...

I smile and remember a love long gone,

reminisce to the sound of that favorite song

While all along I just want to be right, not wrong

Yet my senses long for a strong hand

to take command of this desire

and set my dreams on fire

let them ignite on this late night....

Soulmates Dissipate

My heart aches
as my soul loses a mate
I thought was mine
one of a kind
I was blind
I could not see the irony
Of loving you

I thought it was true
I loved you completely
Loved you deeply
For you to deceive me
And mistreat me

Why does love seem to come
Warm like the sun
Then come undone
Leave you wrung
Out like a towel hung to dry
Asking why didn't I see
We weren't meant to be

Now I hurt and I cry
The tears run from my eyes
Cause I thought for a minute
Your heart was in it

Why should I care
that your love is not there
I was a fool
I've been schooled
Never give your all
You may fall down
look like a clown
when you realize
love was all lies

You say it was true
but who knew
when you live another life
the way you do
I can't understand
How you love another man
like you love me
Couldn't you see
how that would hurt me?

Years went by
nothing was said
You let the feelings
go to my head
Let me dream of us
I put in you my trust

And now you drop the bomb
This love is all wrong
Could never be right
I cannot fight
demons unseen

lusts in between
I never wanted to own you
I just wanted to show you
You meant so much to me
Now I can't see
how I can look you in the eyes
All I see is lies
I despise this pain
This pounding rain
in my heart and mind
How could I be so blind?

Will it ever go away?
You ask me to stay
And be your friend
I want it to end
All this agony trapped inside me
Eats away at my sanity
Drains me of my ability
to see clear
I can't hear
what you're saying
over my heart breaking...

Why did you wait so long?
If you were a man strong enough
to know the choice
why didn't you voice this long ago?
Instead you let me flow,
didn't let me know
this was all show...

When the curtain's drawn
I played the pawn
Take a bow
You have learned how
to kill my soul
Make my world unfold
You've mastered the art
of breaking a heart
Now we're finished
What's left is a blemish
on my soul
I once was whole...

Code Blue

I died last week

Heard the flat line beep

As you turned to walk away

With the love you said would stay

I loved you from my soul

And you came in and stole

My essence

My strength and presence

In such a short time

Never will you find

Another woman like me

Look in the mirror and see

Yourself for the demon you are

Could have loved me from afar

Instead of hurting me up close

I thought I needed another dose

But I think that my system

Just had a toxic embolism

Blood popped, a heart stopped

Because of you

I wish you could feel as blue

as midnight feels

When a thief stabs you and steals

Your last dollar

Don't it make you wanna holler?

But my mouth wouldn't open

I was ready and hoping

One scream and shout

And all of you would pour out of my body

No longer would I be in a trance

Or this f-d up circumstance

Of having been misled

Then left for dead

On the side of love's highway

You're lucky vengeance is not my way

of handling this

One day you'll find the one who fits

But God is one who never forgets

I'll still be around to watch you cry

When your heart is hung out to dry.

All That is Left is a Dream

I looked at you today
and realized I don't know you
Oh, I know who you say you are
But not the real you
I know you have ambitions and goals
Dreams for your future, dreams for our future
Yet I had a dream...

I had a dream that
I met the man God chose for me...
A tall drink of water
who could quench the thirsts of the Sahara.

He dug me, and I dug him;
I sought him out and he eagerly accepted
My quest for love,
A rebirth to a life of mundane experiences.

We courted, went on long drives at night,
Talked about our past and connected
at some deeper level
Time passed and we were committed,
Determined to beat the odds of young love.
I knew where I was going in life
My accomplishments were set in my mind
as a force which drove me to achieve,
And help you to reach your aspirations.

We were devoted to each other
And the new seed we sowed together...

Then, I woke and realized it was just a dream...

In actuality, I chose to take free will
and jump into a pit
Filled with insecurities, false hopes and untruths.
As years went on,
I sank deeper into the pit
Wondering how to get out

I was caught being a mother to a son
Not yet ready for the world;
A son nurtured by a strong, black woman
who depended on his presence to survive;
Entangled in the arms of a man
Incapable of independence,
Sucking and draining the life blood of my soul;
Causing me to become someone I didn't know.
All the love we had could not replace or repair our foundation,
A foundation build on the excitement of life,
rather than the presence of God.

As I look at you now,
I look at a stranger
Who I took into my inner self
And shared my soul with...
I look at what I thought was my all
And see that nothing is left of what once was...

All that is left is a dream...

Acknowledgments

Once again I come with a grateful heart for God's blessings to be able to write and bring joy to someone else. Thank you to my sister, Brandy, who encouraged me to publish this work. You pushed me into purpose and I love you for it. Thank you to my family - especially my mom and daughter, who are my biggest supporters! Thank you to my circle of authentic friends who always encourage one another to become greater. You all are my inspiration.

About the Author

Jeanine Rogers, a Chicago native, was raised by a single mother who nurtured her first loves – faith and family. At the age of 11, she discovered her passion for writing poems and stories, including coauthoring a children's book in high school and interviewing Gwendolyn Brooks, which fueled her passion as she realized the power to transform lives one word at a time.

Dealing with life's obstacles Jeanine overcame the challenges she saw firsthand by learning to remain purposeful and driven. She applied the values planted in her youth and became a scholar who went on to obtain a bachelor's and two masters in education. With 23 years of experience, Jeanine strives to lead the way in encouraging others to become lifelong learners of self.

A woman of action, she balances her career, the joys of being a mom, being an entrepreneur, and teaching English as an adjunct professor, with her writing passion. In her first novel, *Don't Smell Like Smoke, A Novel and Self-Reflection Journal*, Jeanine encourages, inspires, and empowers readers to see themselves as triumphant. This is her second body of work and she plans to continue writing and publishing, both for herself and others, through her consulting company 5 Point Vision, LLC.